# This Maid Of Honor Organizer Belongs To:

_____

# Important Dates At A Glance

Wedding Date _____

Save The Date Mailing By _____

Coordinate Gift Registry _____

Dress Shopping _____

Meeting With Caterer _____

Invitations Mailed By _____

Bridal Shower _____

Final Dress Alterations _____

Finalize Guest List _____

Bachelorette Party _____

Wedding Day Hair/Nails _____

# Master To-Do List

☐ _____
☐ _____
☐ _____
☐ _____
☐ _____
☐ _____
☐ _____
☐ _____
☐ _____
☐ _____
☐ _____
☐ _____
☐ _____
☐ _____
☐ _____
☐ _____
☐ _____

☐ _____
☐ _____
☐ _____
☐ _____
☐ _____
☐ _____
☐ _____
☐ _____
☐ _____
☐ _____
☐ _____
☐ _____
☐ _____
☐ _____
☐ _____
☐ _____
☐ _____

# Monthly Planner

Month Of:_____

| SUN | MON | TUES | WED | THURS | FRI | SAT |
|-----|-----|------|-----|-------|-----|-----|
|     |     |      |     |       |     |     |
|     |     |      |     |       |     |     |
|     |     |      |     |       |     |     |
|     |     |      |     |       |     |     |
|     |     |      |     |       |     |     |

# Monthly *Planner*

## Month Of:_____

| SUN | MON | TUES | WED | THURS | FRI | SAT |
|-----|-----|------|-----|-------|-----|-----|
|     |     |      |     |       |     |     |
|     |     |      |     |       |     |     |
|     |     |      |     |       |     |     |
|     |     |      |     |       |     |     |
|     |     |      |     |       |     |     |

# Monthly *Planner*

## Month Of:_____

| SUN | MON | TUES | WED | THURS | FRI | SAT |
|-----|-----|------|-----|-------|-----|-----|
|     |     |      |     |       |     |     |
|     |     |      |     |       |     |     |
|     |     |      |     |       |     |     |
|     |     |      |     |       |     |     |
|     |     |      |     |       |     |     |

# Monthly Planner

Month Of:_____

| SUN | MON | TUES | WED | THURS | FRI | SAT |
|-----|-----|------|-----|-------|-----|-----|
|     |     |      |     |       |     |     |
|     |     |      |     |       |     |     |
|     |     |      |     |       |     |     |
|     |     |      |     |       |     |     |
|     |     |      |     |       |     |     |

# Monthly Planner

## Month Of:_____

| SUN | MON | TUES | WED | THURS | FRI | SAT |
|-----|-----|------|-----|-------|-----|-----|
|     |     |      |     |       |     |     |
|     |     |      |     |       |     |     |
|     |     |      |     |       |     |     |
|     |     |      |     |       |     |     |
|     |     |      |     |       |     |     |

# Monthly *Planner*

Month Of:_____

| SUN | MON | TUES | WED | THURS | FRI | SAT |
|-----|-----|------|-----|-------|-----|-----|
|     |     |      |     |       |     |     |
|     |     |      |     |       |     |     |
|     |     |      |     |       |     |     |
|     |     |      |     |       |     |     |
|     |     |      |     |       |     |     |

# Weekly Planner

| Sunday | Week Of: _____ |
|---|---|
| Monday | **To Do List:** |
| Tuesday | ☐ _____ |
| Wednesday | ☐ _____ |
| Thursday | ☐ _____ |
| Friday | ☐ _____ |
| Saturday | ☐ _____ |

**APPOINTMENTS**

| Date | Time | Vendor | Contact Info |
|---|---|---|---|
| | | | |
| | | | |
| | | | |
| | | | |

**Notes**

# Weekly Planner

| Sunday |
| --- |
| |

| Monday |
| --- |
| |

| Tuesday |
| --- |
| |

| Wednesday |
| --- |
| |

| Thursday |
| --- |
| |

| Friday |
| --- |
| |

| Saturday |
| --- |
| |

Week Of:_____

## To Do List:

- [ ] 
- [ ] 
- [ ] 
- [ ] 
- [ ] 

## APPOINTMENTS

| Date | Time | Vendor | Contact Info |
| --- | --- | --- | --- |
| | | | |
| | | | |
| | | | |
| | | | |

## Notes

# Weekly Planner

## Sunday

## Monday

## Tuesday

## Wednesday

## Thursday

## Friday

## Saturday

Week Of:_____

### To Do List:

☐

☐

☐

☐

☐

### APPOINTMENTS

| Date | Time | Vendor | Contact Info |
|------|------|--------|--------------|
|      |      |        |              |
|      |      |        |              |
|      |      |        |              |
|      |      |        |              |

### Notes

# Weekly Planner

| Sunday |
| --- |
| |

| Monday |
| --- |
| |

| Tuesday |
| --- |
| |

| Wednesday |
| --- |
| |

| Thursday |
| --- |
| |

| Friday |
| --- |
| |

| Saturday |
| --- |
| |

Week Of:_____

## To Do List:

- [ ]
- [ ]
- [ ]
- [ ]
- [ ]

## APPOINTMENTS

| Date | Time | Vendor | Contact Info |
| --- | --- | --- | --- |
| | | | |
| | | | |
| | | | |
| | | | |

## Notes

| |
| --- |
| |
| |
| |
| |

# Weekly Planner

| Sunday | |
| --- | --- |
| **Monday** | |
| **Tuesday** | |
| **Wednesday** | |
| **Thursday** | |
| **Friday** | |
| **Saturday** | |

Week Of:_____

### To Do List:

- ☐ _____
- ☐ _____
- ☐ _____
- ☐ _____
- ☐ _____

### APPOINTMENTS

| Date | Time | Vendor | Contact Info |
| --- | --- | --- | --- |
| | | | |
| | | | |
| | | | |
| | | | |

### Notes

# Weekly Planner

| Sunday | Week Of: _____ |
| --- | --- |

## To Do List:

☐ _____
☐ _____
☐ _____
☐ _____
☐ _____

**Monday**

**Tuesday**

## APPOINTMENTS

| Date | Time | Vendor | Contact Info |
| --- | --- | --- | --- |
| | | | |
| | | | |
| | | | |
| | | | |

**Wednesday**

**Thursday**

## Notes

_____

_____

_____

_____

_____

**Friday**

**Saturday**

# Weekly Planner

| Sunday | Week Of: _____ |

**Sunday**

**Monday**

**Tuesday**

**Wednesday**

**Thursday**

**Friday**

**Saturday**

## To Do List:

- ☐
- ☐
- ☐
- ☐
- ☐

## APPOINTMENTS

| Date | Time | Vendor | Contact Info |
|------|------|--------|--------------|
|      |      |        |              |
|      |      |        |              |
|      |      |        |              |
|      |      |        |              |

## Notes

# Weekly Planner

| Sunday |
|---|
| |

| Monday |
|---|
| |

| Tuesday |
|---|
| |

| Wednesday |
|---|
| |

| Thursday |
|---|
| |

| Friday |
|---|
| |

| Saturday |
|---|
| |

Week Of:_____

## To Do List:

- ☐
- ☐
- ☐
- ☐
- ☐

## APPOINTMENTS

| Date | Time | Vendor | Contact Info |
|---|---|---|---|
| | | | |
| | | | |
| | | | |
| | | | |

## Notes

# Weekly Planner

| Sunday | |
|---|---|
| **Monday** | |
| **Tuesday** | |
| **Wednesday** | |
| **Thursday** | |
| **Friday** | |
| **Saturday** | |

**Week Of:**_____

## To Do List:

- ☐
- ☐
- ☐
- ☐
- ☐

## APPOINTMENTS

| Date | Time | Vendor | Contact Info |
|---|---|---|---|
| | | | |
| | | | |
| | | | |
| | | | |

## Notes

# Weekly Planner

| Sunday | Week Of:_____ |

**Sunday**

**Monday**

**Tuesday**

**Wednesday**

**Thursday**

**Friday**

**Saturday**

### To Do List:

☐ _____
☐ _____
☐ _____
☐ _____
☐ _____

### APPOINTMENTS

| Date | Time | Vendor | Contact Info |
|------|------|--------|--------------|
|      |      |        |              |
|      |      |        |              |
|      |      |        |              |
|      |      |        |              |

### Notes

# Weekly Planner

## Sunday

## Monday

## Tuesday

## Wednesday

## Thursday

## Friday

## Saturday

Week Of:_____

### To Do List:

- [ ] 
- [ ] 
- [ ] 
- [ ] 
- [ ] 

### APPOINTMENTS

| Date | Time | Vendor | Contact Info |
|------|------|--------|--------------|
|      |      |        |              |
|      |      |        |              |
|      |      |        |              |
|      |      |        |              |

### Notes

# Weekly Planner

| | |
|---|---|
| Sunday | |
| Monday | |
| Tuesday | |
| Wednesday | |
| Thursday | |
| Friday | |
| Saturday | |

Week Of:_____

## To Do List:

- [ ] 
- [ ] 
- [ ] 
- [ ] 
- [ ] 

## APPOINTMENTS

| Date | Time | Vendor | Contact Info |
|------|------|--------|--------------|
|      |      |        |              |
|      |      |        |              |
|      |      |        |              |
|      |      |        |              |

## Notes

# Weekly Planner

| | |
|---|---|
| Sunday | Week Of:_____ |

## To Do List:

- ☐ _____
- ☐ _____
- ☐ _____
- ☐ _____
- ☐ _____

**Monday**

**Tuesday**

## APPOINTMENTS

| Date | Time | Vendor | Contact Info |
|------|------|--------|--------------|
| | | | |
| | | | |
| | | | |
| | | | |

**Wednesday**

**Thursday**

## Notes

**Friday**

**Saturday**

# Weekly Planner

| Sunday |
| --- |

| Monday |
| --- |

| Tuesday |
| --- |

| Wednesday |
| --- |

| Thursday |
| --- |

| Friday |
| --- |

| Saturday |
| --- |

Week Of:_____

## To Do List:

- ☐
- ☐
- ☐
- ☐
- ☐

## APPOINTMENTS

| Date | Time | Vendor | Contact Info |
| --- | --- | --- | --- |
|  |  |  |  |
|  |  |  |  |
|  |  |  |  |
|  |  |  |  |

## Notes

# Weekly Planner

| Sunday |
| --- |
| |

| Monday |
| --- |
| |

| Tuesday |
| --- |
| |

| Wednesday |
| --- |
| |

| Thursday |
| --- |
| |

| Friday |
| --- |
| |

| Saturday |
| --- |
| |

Week Of:_____

## To Do List:

- ☐
- ☐
- ☐
- ☐
- ☐

## APPOINTMENTS

| Date | Time | Vendor | Contact Info |
| --- | --- | --- | --- |
| | | | |
| | | | |
| | | | |
| | | | |

## Notes

# Weekly Planner

| Sunday | Week Of:_____ |

**Sunday**

**Monday**

**Tuesday**

**Wednesday**

**Thursday**

**Friday**

**Saturday**

## To Do List:

☐
☐
☐
☐
☐

## APPOINTMENTS

| Date | Time | Vendor | Contact Info |
|------|------|--------|--------------|
|      |      |        |              |
|      |      |        |              |
|      |      |        |              |
|      |      |        |              |

## Notes

# Weekly Planner

| Sunday |
| --- |
| |

| Monday |
| --- |
| |

| Tuesday |
| --- |
| |

| Wednesday |
| --- |
| |

| Thursday |
| --- |
| |

| Friday |
| --- |
| |

| Saturday |
| --- |
| |

Week Of:_____

## To Do List:

- ☐
- ☐
- ☐
- ☐
- ☐

## APPOINTMENTS

| Date | Time | Vendor | Contact Info |
| --- | --- | --- | --- |
| | | | |
| | | | |
| | | | |
| | | | |

## Notes

| |
| --- |
| |
| |
| |
| |

# Weekly Planner

| Sunday | Week Of: _____ |

**Sunday**

**Monday**

**Tuesday**

**Wednesday**

**Thursday**

**Friday**

**Saturday**

## To Do List:

☐ _____
☐ _____
☐ _____
☐ _____
☐ _____

## APPOINTMENTS

| Date | Time | Vendor | Contact Info |
|------|------|--------|--------------|
|      |      |        |              |
|      |      |        |              |
|      |      |        |              |
|      |      |        |              |

## Notes

# Weekly Planner

| Sunday | |
| --- | --- |
| Monday | |
| Tuesday | |
| Wednesday | |
| Thursday | |
| Friday | |
| Saturday | |

Week Of:_____

## To Do List:

- ☐
- ☐
- ☐
- ☐
- ☐

## APPOINTMENTS

| Date | Time | Vendor | Contact Info |
| --- | --- | --- | --- |
| | | | |
| | | | |
| | | | |
| | | | |

## Notes

# Weekly Planner

| Sunday |
| --- |
| |

| Monday |
| --- |
| |

| Tuesday |
| --- |
| |

| Wednesday |
| --- |
| |

| Thursday |
| --- |
| |

| Friday |
| --- |
| |

| Saturday |
| --- |
| |

Week Of:_____

## To Do List:

- ☐
- ☐
- ☐
- ☐
- ☐

## APPOINTMENTS

| Date | Time | Vendor | Contact Info |
| --- | --- | --- | --- |
| | | | |
| | | | |
| | | | |
| | | | |

## Notes

# Weekly Planner

## Sunday

## Monday

## Tuesday

## Wednesday

## Thursday

## Friday

## Saturday

Week Of:_____

### To Do List:

- ☐
- ☐
- ☐
- ☐
- ☐

### APPOINTMENTS

| Date | Time | Vendor | Contact Info |
|------|------|--------|--------------|
|      |      |        |              |
|      |      |        |              |
|      |      |        |              |
|      |      |        |              |

### Notes

# Weekly Planner

| Sunday | |
|---|---|

**Week Of:**_____

## To Do List:

☐ _____
☐ _____
☐ _____
☐ _____
☐ _____

| Monday | |
|---|---|

| Tuesday | |
|---|---|

### APPOINTMENTS

| Date | Time | Vendor | Contact Info |
|---|---|---|---|
| | | | |
| | | | |
| | | | |
| | | | |

| Wednesday | |
|---|---|

| Thursday | |
|---|---|

### Notes

| Friday | |
|---|---|

| Saturday | |
|---|---|

# Weekly Planner

## Sunday

## Monday

## Tuesday

## Wednesday

## Thursday

## Friday

## Saturday

Week Of:_____

### To Do List:

☐

☐

☐

☐

☐

### APPOINTMENTS

| Date | Time | Vendor | Contact Info |
|------|------|--------|--------------|
|      |      |        |              |
|      |      |        |              |
|      |      |        |              |
|      |      |        |              |

### Notes

# Weekly Planner

| | |
|---|---|
| **Sunday** | **Week Of:** _____ |

## Sunday

## Monday

## Tuesday

## Wednesday

## Thursday

## Friday

## Saturday

### To Do List:

☐
☐
☐
☐
☐

### APPOINTMENTS

| Date | Time | Vendor | Contact Info |
|------|------|--------|--------------|
|      |      |        |              |
|      |      |        |              |
|      |      |        |              |
|      |      |        |              |

### Notes

# Weekly Planner

| Sunday | Week Of:_____ |

**Sunday**

**Monday**

**Tuesday**

**Wednesday**

**Thursday**

**Friday**

**Saturday**

## To Do List:

☐
☐
☐
☐
☐

## APPOINTMENTS

| Date | Time | Vendor | Contact Info |
|------|------|--------|--------------|
|      |      |        |              |
|      |      |        |              |
|      |      |        |              |
|      |      |        |              |

## Notes

# Weekly Planner

| Sunday | Week Of:_____ |

**Sunday**

**Monday**

**Tuesday**

**Wednesday**

**Thursday**

**Friday**

**Saturday**

## To Do List:

- ☐
- ☐
- ☐
- ☐
- ☐

## APPOINTMENTS

| Date | Time | Vendor | Contact Info |
|------|------|--------|--------------|
|      |      |        |              |
|      |      |        |              |
|      |      |        |              |
|      |      |        |              |

## Notes

# Weekly Planner

| Sunday |
|---|
| |

| Monday |
|---|
| |

| Tuesday |
|---|
| |

| Wednesday |
|---|
| |

| Thursday |
|---|
| |

| Friday |
|---|
| |

| Saturday |
|---|
| |

Week Of:_____

## To Do List:

- ☐
- ☐
- ☐
- ☐
- ☐

## APPOINTMENTS

| Date | Time | Vendor | Contact Info |
|---|---|---|---|
| | | | |
| | | | |
| | | | |
| | | | |

## Notes

# Weekly Planner

| Sunday | Week Of:_____ |
|---|---|

**Sunday**

**Monday**

**Tuesday**

**Wednesday**

**Thursday**

**Friday**

**Saturday**

## To Do List:

☐ _____
☐ _____
☐ _____
☐ _____
☐ _____

## APPOINTMENTS

| Date | Time | Vendor | Contact Info |
|---|---|---|---|
| | | | |
| | | | |
| | | | |
| | | | |

## Notes

# Weekly Planner

| Sunday |
| --- |
|  |

| Monday |
| --- |
|  |

| Tuesday |
| --- |
|  |

| Wednesday |
| --- |
|  |

| Thursday |
| --- |
|  |

| Friday |
| --- |
|  |

| Saturday |
| --- |
|  |

Week Of:_____

## To Do List:

- ☐
- ☐
- ☐
- ☐
- ☐

## APPOINTMENTS

| Date | Time | Vendor | Contact Info |
| --- | --- | --- | --- |
|  |  |  |  |
|  |  |  |  |
|  |  |  |  |
|  |  |  |  |

## Notes

# Weekly Planner

| Sunday |
| --- |
| |

| Monday |
| --- |
| |

| Tuesday |
| --- |
| |

| Wednesday |
| --- |
| |

| Thursday |
| --- |
| |

| Friday |
| --- |
| |

| Saturday |
| --- |
| |

Week Of:_____

## To Do List:

☐ _____
☐ _____
☐ _____
☐ _____
☐ _____

## APPOINTMENTS

| Date | Time | Vendor | Contact Info |
| --- | --- | --- | --- |
| | | | |
| | | | |
| | | | |
| | | | |

## Notes

_____
_____
_____
_____

# Bridal Party Contact List

Name:

Cell:

Email:

Role:


Name:

Cell:

Email:

Role:


Name:

Cell:

Email:

Role:


Name:

Cell:

Email:

Role:


Name:

Cell:

Email:

Role:


Name:

Cell:

Email:

Role:


Name:

Cell:

Email:

Role:


Name:

Cell:

Email:

Role:


Name:

Cell:

Email:

Role:


Name:

Cell:

Email:

Role:

# Bridal Party Contact List

Name:

Cell:

Email:

Role:


Name:

Cell:

Email:

Role:


Name:

Cell:

Email:

Role:


Name:

Cell:

Email:

Role:


Name:

Cell:

Email:

Role:


Name:

Cell:

Email:

Role:


Name:

Cell:

Email:

Role:


Name:

Cell:

Email:

Role:


Name:

Cell:

Email:

Role:


Name:

Cell:

Email:

Role:

# Vendor Contact List

## WEDDING CAKE

Vendor:

Contact:

Email:

Phone:

Notes:

## CEREMONY VENUE

Vendor:

Contact:

Email:

Phone:

Notes:

## RECEPTION ENTERTAINMENT

Vendor:

Contact:

Email:

Phone:

Notes:

## RECEPTION VENUE

Vendor:

Contact:

Email:

Phone:

Notes:

# Vendor Contact List

## BACHELORETTE PARTY VENUE

Vendor:

Contact:

Email:

Phone:

Notes:

## WEDDING HAIR

Vendor:

Contact:

Email:

Phone:

Notes:

## WEDDING NAILS

Vendor:

Contact:

Email:

Phone:

Notes:

## CEREMONY OFFICIANT

Vendor:

Contact:

Email:

Phone:

Notes:

# Vendor Contact List

## FLORIST

Vendor:

Contact:

Email:

Phone:

Notes:

## CATERER

Vendor:

Contact:

Email:

Phone:

Notes:

## EM CEE

Vendor:

Contact:

Email:

Phone:

Notes:

## LIMO/TRANSPORTATION

Vendor:

Contact:

Email:

Phone:

Notes:

# Vendor Contact List

## WEDDING COORDINATOR

Vendor:

Contact:

Email:

Phone:

Notes:

## PHOTOGRAPHER

Vendor:

Contact:

Email:

Phone:

Notes:

## VIDEOGRAPHER

Vendor:

Contact:

Email:

Phone:

Notes:

## ALTERATIONS

Vendor:

Contact:

Email:

Phone:

Notes:

# Vendor Contact List

Vendor: _____     Vendor: _____

Contact: _____     Contact: _____

Email: _____     Email: _____

Phone: _____     Phone: _____

Notes: _____     Notes: _____

_____     _____

_____     _____

_____     _____

_____     _____

Vendor: _____     Vendor: _____

Contact: _____     Contact: _____

Email: _____     Email: _____

Phone: _____     Phone: _____

Notes: _____     Notes: _____

_____     _____

_____     _____

_____     _____

# Vendor Contact List

Vendor: _____

Contact: _____

Email: _____

Phone: _____

Notes: _____

_____

_____

_____

_____

Vendor: _____

Contact: _____

Email: _____

Phone: _____

Notes: _____

_____

_____

_____

_____

Vendor: _____

Contact: _____

Email: _____

Phone: _____

Notes: _____

_____

_____

_____

_____

Vendor: _____

Contact: _____

Email: _____

Phone: _____

Notes: _____

_____

_____

_____

_____

# Bridal Shower **Budget**

## Total Budget

| CATEGORY | BUDGET | ACTUAL COST | DEPOSIT PAID | BALANCE | DUE |
|---|---|---|---|---|---|
| **INVITATIONS** | | | | | |
| Save The Date | | | | | |
| Invitations | | | | | |
| Envelopes | | | | | |
| Thank You Cards | | | | | |
| Postage | | | | | |
| | | | | | |
| **VENUE** | | | | | |
| Rental Fee | | | | | |
| Misc. | | | | | |
| | | | | | |
| **FOOD & DRINK** | | | | | |
| Catering | | | | | |
| Beverages | | | | | |
| Alcoholic | | | | | |
| Non-alcoholic | | | | | |
| Cake | | | | | |
| Plates/Bowls | | | | | |
| Utensils | | | | | |
| Napkins | | | | | |
| | | | | | |

# Bridal Shower Budget

| CATEGORY | BUDGET | ACTUAL COST | DEPOSIT PAID | BALANCE | DUE |
|---|---|---|---|---|---|
| **DECORATIONS** | | | | | |
| Table Decorations | | | | | |
| Venue Decorations | | | | | |
| Signs, Banners, Wall Decor | | | | | |
| Misc. Decorations | | | | | |
| | | | | | |
| **FAVORS & GAMES** | | | | | |
| **Games** | | | | | |
| Prizes | | | | | |
| Favors | | | | | |
| | | | | | |
| **ENTERTAINMENT** | | | | | |
| | | | | | |
| | | | | | |
| | | | | | |
| **OTHER** | | | | | |
| | | | | | |
| | | | | | |
| | | | | | |
| | | | | | |
| | | | | | |

# Bridal Shower Planner

| PARTY DETAILS |
| --- |
| DATE |
| TIME |
| VENUE |
| THEME |
| NOTES |
|  |

| GAMES/ACTIVITIES |
| --- |
|  |
|  |
|  |
|  |
|  |

## Food/Drink

## Decorations

| GUEST LIST | | |
|---|---|---|
| NAME | CONTACT INFO | RSVP |
|  |  |  |
|  |  |  |
|  |  |  |
|  |  |  |
|  |  |  |
|  |  |  |
|  |  |  |
|  |  |  |
|  |  |  |
|  |  |  |
|  |  |  |
|  |  |  |
|  |  |  |
|  |  |  |
|  |  |  |
|  |  |  |
|  |  |  |
|  |  |  |
|  |  |  |
|  |  |  |
|  |  |  |

| GUEST LIST | | |
|---|---|---|
| NAME | CONTACT INFO | RSVP |
| | | |
| | | |
| | | |
| | | |
| | | |
| | | |
| | | |
| | | |
| | | |
| | | |
| | | |
| | | |
| | | |
| | | |
| | | |
| | | |
| | | |
| | | |
| | | |
| | | |

# Shopping List

- [ ] _____
- [ ] _____
- [ ] _____
- [ ] _____
- [ ] _____
- [ ] _____
- [ ] _____
- [ ] _____
- [ ] _____
- [ ] _____
- [ ] _____
- [ ] _____
- [ ] _____
- [ ] _____
- [ ] _____
- [ ] _____
- [ ] _____

- [ ] _____
- [ ] _____
- [ ] _____
- [ ] _____
- [ ] _____
- [ ] _____
- [ ] _____
- [ ] _____
- [ ] _____
- [ ] _____
- [ ] _____
- [ ] _____
- [ ] _____
- [ ] _____
- [ ] _____
- [ ] _____
- [ ] _____

# Bachelorette Party Budget

## Total Budget

| CATEGORY | BUDGET | ACTUAL COST | DEPOSIT PAID | BALANCE | DUE |
|---|---|---|---|---|---|
| **INVITATIONS** | | | | | |
| Save The Date | | | | | |
| Invitations | | | | | |
| Envelopes | | | | | |
| Thank You Cards | | | | | |
| Postage | | | | | |
| | | | | | |
| **VENUE** | | | | | |
| Rental Fee | | | | | |
| Misc. | | | | | |
| | | | | | |
| **FOOD & DRINK** | | | | | |
| Catering | | | | | |
| Beverages | | | | | |
|    Alcoholic | | | | | |
|    Non-alcoholic | | | | | |
| Cake | | | | | |
| Plates/Bowls | | | | | |
| Utensils | | | | | |
| Napkins | | | | | |
| | | | | | |

# Bachelorette Party Budget

| CATEGORY | BUDGET | ACTUAL COST | DEPOSIT PAID | BALANCE | DUE |
|---|---|---|---|---|---|
| **DECORATIONS** | | | | | |
| Table Decorations | | | | | |
| Venue Decorations | | | | | |
| Signs, Banners, Wall Decor | | | | | |
| Misc. Decorations | | | | | |
| | | | | | |
| **FAVORS & GAMES** | | | | | |
| **Games** | | | | | |
| Prizes | | | | | |
| Favors | | | | | |
| | | | | | |
| **ENTERTAINMENT** | | | | | |
| | | | | | |
| | | | | | |
| | | | | | |
| **OTHER** | | | | | |
| | | | | | |
| | | | | | |
| | | | | | |
| | | | | | |
| | | | | | |

# Bachelorette Party Planner

| PARTY DETAILS | |
|---|---|
| DATE | |
| TIME | |
| VENUE | |
| THEME | |
| NOTES | |
| | |

| GAMES/ACTIVITIES |
|---|
| |
| |
| |
| |
| |
| |

## Food/Drink

## Decorations

| GUEST LIST | | |
|---|---|---|
| NAME | CONTACT INFO | RSVP |
| | | |
| | | |
| | | |
| | | |
| | | |
| | | |
| | | |
| | | |
| | | |
| | | |
| | | |
| | | |
| | | |
| | | |
| | | |
| | | |
| | | |
| | | |
| | | |
| | | |
| | | |

| GUEST LIST | | |
|---|---|---|
| NAME | CONTACT INFO | RSVP |
| | | |
| | | |
| | | |
| | | |
| | | |
| | | |
| | | |
| | | |
| | | |
| | | |
| | | |
| | | |
| | | |
| | | |
| | | |
| | | |
| | | |
| | | |
| | | |
| | | |

# Shopping List

- [ ] _____
- [ ] _____
- [ ] _____
- [ ] _____
- [ ] _____
- [ ] _____
- [ ] _____
- [ ] _____
- [ ] _____
- [ ] _____
- [ ] _____
- [ ] _____
- [ ] _____
- [ ] _____
- [ ] _____
- [ ] _____
- [ ] _____

- [ ] _____
- [ ] _____
- [ ] _____
- [ ] _____
- [ ] _____
- [ ] _____
- [ ] _____
- [ ] _____
- [ ] _____
- [ ] _____
- [ ] _____
- [ ] _____
- [ ] _____
- [ ] _____
- [ ] _____
- [ ] _____
- [ ] _____

# Wedding Day Emergency Kit

## Apparel Repair Kit

- [ ] Small Scissors
- [ ] Safety Pins
- [ ] Hem Tape
- [ ] Clear Nail Polish
- [ ] Tide-To-Go
- [ ] Lint Roller
- [ ] Sewing Kit

## Hair

- [ ] Comb/Brush
- [ ] Bobby Pins
- [ ] Hair Ties
- [ ] Hairspray
- [ ] Dry Shampoo
- [ ] Hair Straightener/Curling Iron

## Toiletries

- [ ] Q-Tips
- [ ] Tweezers
- [ ] Nail File
- [ ] Touch-up Nail Polish
- [ ] Deodorant
- [ ] Perfume
- [ ] Tissues
- [ ] Tampons/Pads
- [ ] Toothbrush/Paste/Floss
- [ ] Lotion

## Meds/First Aid

- [ ] Antacid
- [ ] Band-Aids
- [ ] Tylenol/Motrin
- [ ] Contact Solution
- [ ] Allergy Medicine
- [ ] Bug Spray

# Notes/Ideas/Memories

# Notes/Ideas/Memories

# Notes/Ideas/Memories

# Notes/Ideas/Memories

# Notes/Ideas/Memories

# Notes/Ideas/Memories

# Notes/Ideas/Memories

# Notes/Ideas/Memories

# Notes/Ideas/Memories

# Notes/Ideas/Memories

# Notes/Ideas/Memories

# Notes/Ideas/Memories

# Notes/Ideas/Memories

# Notes/Ideas/Memories

# Notes/Ideas/Memories

# Notes/Ideas/Memories

# Notes/Ideas/Memories

# Notes/Ideas/Memories

# Notes/Ideas/Memories

# Notes/Ideas/Memories

# Notes/Ideas/Memories

# Notes/Ideas/Memories

# Notes/Ideas/Memories

# Notes/Ideas/Memories

# Notes/Ideas/Memories

# Notes/Ideas/Memories

# Notes/Ideas/Memories

# Notes/Ideas/Memories

# Notes/Ideas/Memories

# Notes/Ideas/Memories

# Notes/Ideas/Memories

# Notes/Ideas/Memories

# Notes/Ideas/Memories

# Notes/Ideas/Memories

# Notes/Ideas/Memories

# Notes/Ideas/Memories

# Notes/Ideas/Memories

# Notes/Ideas/Memories

# Notes/Ideas/Memories

# Notes/Ideas/Memories

# Notes/Ideas/Memories

# Notes/Ideas/Memories

# Notes/Ideas/Memories

# Notes/Ideas/Memories

# Notes/Ideas/Memories

# Notes/Ideas/Memories

# Notes/Ideas/Memories

# Notes/Ideas/Memories

# Notes/Ideas/Memories

# Notes/Ideas/Memories

CPSIA information can be obtained
at www.ICGtesting.com
Printed in the USA
BVHW050423160421
605034BV00006B/756